NAZI ARCHITECTS
OF THE HOLOCAUST

CORONA BREZINA

ROSEN
PUBLISHING®

New York

Published in 2015 by The Rosen Publishing Group, Inc.
29 East 21st Street, New York, NY 10010

Copyright © 2015 by The Rosen Publishing Group, Inc.

First Edition

Library of Congress Cataloging-in-Publication Data

Brezina, Corona, author.
Nazi architects of the Holocaust/Corona Brezina.
    pages cm. — (A documentary history of the Holocaust)
Includes bibliographical references and index.
ISBN 978-1-4777-7597-4 (library bound)
1. Holocaust, Jewish (1939-1945—Juvenile literature. 2. Jews—Persecutions—
Germany—History—20th century—Juvenile literature. 3. Germany—Politics
and government—1933-1945—Juvenile literature. 4. Germany—Ethnic
relations—History—20th century—Juvenile literature. I. Title.
D804.34.B74 2015
940.53'18—dc23

                                                          2014001217

Manufactured in the United States of America

CONTENTS

INTRODUCTION

Following Reinhard Heydrich's death, the Czech village of Lidice was leveled by the Nazis due to unfounded claims that the assassin had hidden there. Most of the residents were executed or sent to concentration camps.

4

On May 27, 1942, two Czech resistance fighters trained by the British parachuted into Prague. Their mission was to assassinate Reinhard Heydrich, the Nazi leader known as "the blond beast" and "the Hangman of Prague." One of the agents threw a bomb at Heydrich's open-top Mercedes. Seriously injured by shrapnel, Heydrich died of infection on June 3.

Heydrich had been one of the top Nazi leaders involved with planning and implementing the Final Solution, the euphemism for the genocide of Jews and the mass murder of other non-Germans across Europe. His death did not stop the killing. Two death camps had just begun operations in the spring. After the assassination, the extermination effort was given the code name Operation Reinhard. Other top Nazi leaders, including Heinrich Himmler and Adolf Eichmann, continued the work of administering the Final Solution.

The implementation of the Final Solution was ruthless and thorough, but the chain of events that led to the decision of genocide was more convoluted. When World War II broke out in 1939, the Nazis had not yet planned to exterminate the Jews. Their intention was to deport Jews and other non-Germans east beyond the borders of the expanded

German state. But the Nazis learned that the deportation of millions of Jews and other non-Germans was a difficult and complicated process. They discovered that killing was easy.

Little documentation exists regarding the process by which the Nazis arrived at the Final Solution. Adolf Hitler did not put any details about Jewish matters into writing, issuing his orders verbally. Himmler's and Heydrich's files were destroyed. In addition, the Nazis tended to hide their crimes behind euphemisms. The Final Solution only gradually evolved to mean "extermination." Therefore, documents referring to the Final Solution are open to interpretation. For example, does a 1941 document directing Heydrich to devise a "total solution to the Jewish question" refer to absolute genocide, or were deportations still planned for some of the Jewish population? Overall, the topic of precisely when and how the Nazi leadership adopted the Final Solution is still under debate among historians.

The Final Solution involved Hitler and his hatred of the Jews, his underlings who competed with each other for the leader's favor, and legions of Nazis who followed orders unquestioningly as the atrocities became more brutal and commonplace. At every level, from the bureaucrats to the local police forces, the Nazis became more accustomed as the war dragged on to crimes against humanity being perpetrated against the Jews and other non-Germans. But the Final Solution ultimately involved organized, systematic killing rather than spontaneous violence. This methodical, inexorable annihilation was made possible by the work of Heydrich and the other architects of the Holocaust.

A POISONOUS IDEOLOGY

1

In 1919, the Treaty of Versailles formally ended the war between Germany and the Allies. World War I (1914–1918) had been called "the war to end all wars," and the peace settlement was intended to prevent such a horrific conflict from ever occurring again. Instead of bringing order to Germany, however, the terms of the treaty contributed to a period of crisis in the years that followed that war.

Many Germans considered the conditions of the peace settlement to be harsh and blamed it for the nation's economic and political turmoil. Some Germans didn't even want to admit that Germany had lost the war. According to this "stabbed in the back" myth, left-wing elements in the government—including the Jews—had surrendered even though the army could have emerged victorious.

The democratic government, called the Weimar Republic, was too weak to govern effectively. Dire economic conditions left many Germans dissatisfied with the political system. Extremist political groups gained followers, including the right-wing National Socialist German Workers' Party. Better known as the Nazi Party, it was pro-Aryan and anti-Semitic, meaning that they believed that Jews were inherently

Ordinary Germans suffered economic hardship during the 1920s and 1930s, and many people lost their jobs and savings. Here, a child picks through trash in a Berlin marketplace.

inferior to Germans. In such uncertain times, many ordinary Germans were willing to subscribe to an ideology that claimed the superiority of their own race and blamed another group for their problems.

RISE OF THE NAZI PARTY

Adolf Hitler became the leader of the Nazi Party in 1921, shortly after its founding. Hitler blamed the Jews for the defeat in World War I and believed that they were part of an international conspiracy to dominate spheres such as finance and the press.

In 1923, Hitler led an unsuccessful *putsch,* or violent over-throw, of the government of the German state of Bavaria. The attempt resulted in an eight-month prison sentence for Hitler. While he was imprisoned, he dictated a manifesto called *Mein Kampf,* or "My Struggle," to Rudolf Hess, who was a coconspirator. Published in 1925, it presented Hitler's phi-losophy. He railed against the Jews and asserted the superiority of the Aryan race:

> **Look at the ravages from which our people are suffering daily as a result of being contaminated with Jewish blood...Think**

further of how the process of racial decom-
position is debasing and in some cases even
destroying the fundamental Aryan quali-
ties of our German people.

He also condoned discrimination and violence against
Jews:

In times of distress a wave of public anger
has usually arisen against the Jew; the

LEBENSRAUM

As a corollary to Hitler's belief in the racial superiority of Aryans,
he contended that the German people required more *Lebensraum*,
or "living space," as he described in *Mein Kampf*:

The foreign policy of a People's State must
first of all bear in mind the duty of securing
the existence of the race which is incorporated
in this State. And this must be done by estab-
lishing a healthy and natural proportion
between the number and growth of the population on the one hand and the extent and
resources of the territory they inhabit, on the
other...

It ought to be an Eastern policy which will
have in view the acquisition of such territory
as is necessary for our German people.

Specifically, he wanted to expand into Soviet territory. But in
addition to acquiring an empire, it was to be a Germanized
empire. The non-Germans living in the expanded German
homeland had to be expelled. After Hitler came to power, he
began to carry out his brutal plan of expansion as described over
a decade earlier in *Mein Kampf*.

masses have taken the law into their own hands; they have seized Jewish property and ruined the Jew.

Mein Kampf sold well, and the Nazi Party grew rapidly. Nazi candidates won seats in the Reichstag—the German parliament—in 1928 and became the nation's dominant right-wing political force by 1932.

DICTATORSHIP AND THE ROAD TO WAR

In 1933, Hitler was appointed chancellor, the head of the German government. Historians often point out that the Nazi Party never won a majority of the vote in a free election—at most, the party received 37.3 percent of the vote. Nonetheless, Hitler immediately reinforced his authority with an emergency decree that crippled any political opposition. From this point onward, he acted as dictator of Germany.

Hitler immediately began implementing Nazi ideology by imposing discriminatory measures against Jews. Storm troopers—members of the Nazi Party militia—assaulted Jews in the streets in the ensuing days and months. Nazi leaders called for a one-day boycott of Jewish businesses on April 1, 1933. Jews were banned from holding positions in the government and teaching in universities, and further restrictions were relentlessly imposed. Thousands of Jews were sent to concentration camps (these were set up for the purpose of detention; death camps were constructed later) that had been set up after Hitler's ascent. Tens of thousands fled Germany.

In 1935, the Nuremberg Laws made discrimination against Jews the official policy of the Third Reich. An

Holding banners bearing a swastika and the words "Deutschland Erwache" ("Germany Awake"), members of the Nazi Party hold a rally in Munich, a day after Hitler's failed *putsch* in 1923. Strident anti-Semitism was a central tenet of the Nazi ideology from the beginning.

introductory statement emphasized that "the purity of German blood is essential to the further existence of the German people." Among other restrictions, the document prohibited Jews from marrying Germans. An accompanying Reich Citizenship Law stated that only ethnic Germans could hold citizenship. The Nuremberg Laws set the precedent for the legally sanctioned persecution that would culminate in the Holocaust.

Discrimination against Jews worsened after Austria became part of the Third Reich in 1938. New laws restricted their political rights, livelihoods, housing, and property—Jews were gradually forbidden to own items from radios to magazines. Jews started becoming the victims of violence

Cheered on by supporters, Adolf Hitler, holding his hat, leaves the Presidential Palace in Berlin after having been named chancellor of Germany on January 30, 1933.

that culminated in Kristallnacht, or "The Night of Broken Glass," on November 9, 1938. Tens of thousands were arrested and held for months in concentration camps.

In 1939, World War II broke out after the Germans invaded Czechoslovakia and Poland, and the pressure on Jews increased. Their legal rights were further eroded, and food rations were limited. Gypsies, as well as Jews, were increasingly used for forced labor.

BRUTALITY IN THE EAST

The occupation of Czechoslovakia and Poland put the populations of the two formerly sovereign nations—including more than 1.7 million Polish Jews—under German control. The Nazis began extending their racial policies to the newly occupied territories. Especially in Poland, the excesses of Nazi brutality exceeded the harshness of the measures that had been implemented within Germany. Many German citizens were still ambivalent about Nazi extremism. In faraway Poland, the German invaders found themselves under few restraints.

During the autumn of 1939, the Germans lacked any unified policy for governing Poland. High officers of the Wehrmacht, the regular German army, intended to set up a stable administration. Nazi leaders had their own agenda. They began making secret plans for placing some of Poland's leaders and intelligentsia in internment camps and deporting others. Poland's Jews would be confined to ghettos and eventually deported and resettled elsewhere. The general population would be kept subjugated.

In the meantime, before systematic measures could be implemented, Poland was subjected to a chaotic period of terror. In addition to the army, Einsatzgruppen—"action groups," or mobile task forces, participated in the pacification of Poland. Reinhard Heydrich described their task as "Fundamental cleansing: Jews, intelligentsia, clergy, nobles," as quoted in Christopher Browning's *The Origins of the Final Solution*. They were charged with arresting thirty thousand people and shipping them to concentration camps. Mass shootings of civilians, eventually numbering in the tens of thousands, were carried out at the hands of the Einsatzgruppen along with members of the army and the police. As the fall commenced, a greater number of the victims were Jewish. The Nazis would learn from this period that murder provided a simple means of implementing their racial policies, although they had not yet conceived of systematic extermination.

CHAPTER 2

HITLER'S HENCHMEN

Adolf Hitler laid down his racial ideology in *Mein Kampf*, but he left the details of implementing his doctrines to his subordinates. Following the annexation of Polish territory in 1939, high-ranking Nazi leaders began wrangling over how the new territory should be administered and exploited. Top army officials initially attempted to restrain Nazi extremism, but they turned their attention away from Poland as the war effort escalated elsewhere in Europe.

Certain areas of Poland were incorporated into the Third Reich, and remaining territory in occupied Poland was placed under the administration of Hans Frank. The high-ranking Nazi leader Heinrich Himmler began an ambitious plan of population redistribution. He was charged with two roles: deporting non-Germans and resettling ethnic Germans from Eastern Europe in incorporated territory. Ultimately, he planned the deportation of 5.6 million Poles and more than 500,000 Jews.

Himmler's plan did not proceed smoothly. The logistics proved unworkable, from the difficulties of managing housing to a lack of trains for transfer. In addition, other high-ranking Nazis opposed his

Polish Jews being deported from Warsaw are loaded onto cattle cars of a train. Deportees received no food or water during the transport, and many died before reaching their destination.

actions. Hermann Göring, who was largely responsible for the German economy, held that the Polish manpower was needed in the incorporated territory for agricultural production. Frank objected to the massive influx of population being deported into his jurisdiction. Alternate plans were proposed, such as transporting all of the Jews to Madagascar. In early 1941, as the Germans began preparing to invade the Soviet Union, some top Nazis considered eventually expelling Jews into Soviet territories.

The idea of mass exterminations had not yet been proposed. But three men already involved in the deportation and resettlement attempt—Heinrich Himmler, Reinhard

Heydrich, and Adolf Eichmann—would eventually become the primary coordinators of the Final Solution.

HEINRICH HIMMLER

Heinrich Himmler was born in 1900 in Munich, the capital of Bavaria. World War I broke out in 1914, and Himmler began military training in 1915. He hoped to see action in battle as an officer, but the war ended in 1918 before he was sent to the front. As with many men of his generation, Himmler's experiences during the war, defeat, and aftermath profoundly shaped his worldview. In 1923, he took part in Hitler's attempt to take over the Bavarian government.

Himmler's political activities increased, and he traveled extensively giving speeches on behalf of the Nazi Party. He became involved in the SS (Schutzstaffel, or "protection squad") in 1925 and rose in the ranks as he took on more command duties, becoming head of the organization in 1929. Under his leadership, the SS grew from a few hundred members to an elite security force of more than forty thousand members by 1932. The SS was responsible for administering and implementing the Final Solution as well as other acts later deemed to be crimes against humanity.

After the formation of the Nazi government in 1933, Himmler took on more powerful roles. He was named commander of the Bavarian political police, which gave him considerable authority to order arrests. He "made extensive use of protective custody," as he stated in a March press conference, and established the first concentration camp in Dachau, near Munich, later in the month. Dachau would serve as a model for subsequent Nazi concentration camps.

By 1935, Himmler had been named chief of German police of all Germany. His control extended to the Geheime

Heinrich Himmler *(center)* attends roll call of an SS group in Berlin. During the 1930s, Himmler was instrumental in shaping the SS, which he viewed as an elite force.

Staatspolizei—the "Secret State Police," better known as the Gestapo, in addition to the SS. Beginning in 1937, he began a massive expansion of the concentration camp system in expectation that war would break out. In 1939, he established the Waffen SS, which were armed units, and the Einsatzgruppen. SS membership surged after the war began.

After the invasion of Poland, Himmler took on the title of Reich Commissar for the Consolidation of the Ethnic German Nation. As the resettlement projects proved difficult to engineer, deportations would gradually give way to mass murder.

REINHARD HEYDRICH

Reinhard Heydrich was born in the German state of Saxony in 1904. He joined the navy in 1922 and received a dishonorable discharge in 1931 as a result of a scandal involving the daughter of a senior officer. He was immediately hired by Himmler to organize a security division within the SS. Heydrich became Himmler's trusted subordinate and close friend. Himmler tended to develop ideology and strategy, which Heydrich would implement as policy.

Heydrich's security service, the SD, quickly grew into a formidable intelligence agency. Heydrich maintained

Reinhard Heydrich *(center left)* ascends the steps to Prague Castle. After being appointed Reich Protector in 1941, he oversaw a reign of terror that crushed the Czech resistance movement.

leadership of the SD while consolidating his authority over security agencies. He became head of the Gestapo in 1934, and later of the Security Police Main Office, which incorporated the Gestapo and Kripo, the German criminal police. In 1939, he was named head of the powerful new department, the Reich Security Main Office (RSHA), which joined the SD and the Security Police. Heydrich was also responsible for organizing and deploying the Einsatzgruppen.

Heydrich's various security forces were instrumental in carrying out the Reich's anti-Jewish policies, and Heydrich himself played a key role in the development of the Final Solution. In 1939, Hermann Göring charged Heydrich with drafting a "solution to the Jewish Question" in German territory. At this point, the plan was to expel the Jews into conquered Soviet territory. But in mid-1941, Göring gave Heydrich a new assignment, as quoted in Lucy Dawidowicz's *The War Against the Jews 1933–1945*:

> **As a supplement to the task that was entrusted to you in the decree dated January 24, 1939, namely, to solve the Jewish question by emigration and evacuation in the most favorable way possible, given present conditions, I herewith commission you to carry out all necessary preparations with regard to organizational, substantive, and financial viewpoints for a total solution of the Jewish question in the German sphere of influence in Europe.**

Historians are still debating whether Heydrich interpreted this document as granting authority to draft plans for the total extermination of the Jews. Nonetheless, Heydrich's subsequent actions would facilitate the unprecedented genocide that began in 1942.

HEYDRICH ON THE "JEWISH QUESTION"

Three weeks after the invasion of Poland, Heydrich wrote a letter describing the "concentration" of Jews into ghettos.

To: <u>**Chiefs of all Einsatzgruppen of the Security Police**</u>

<u>**Regarding:**</u> **Jewish Question in Occupied Territory**

I refer to the discussion which took place today in Berlin and point out once more, that the <u>**planned overall measures**</u> **(that is, the final objective) are to be kept** <u>**strictly secret**</u>**...**

<u>**As first prerequisite for the final objective ranks above all the concentration of the Jews from the countryside into the larger cities**</u>**...**

A fundamental principle is that Jewish communities with <u>**fewer than 500**</u> **people are to be dissolved and conveyed to the nearest concentration city...**

In each Jewish community a Jewish Council of Elders is to be set up...It is to be made literally <u>**completely responsible**</u> **for the implementation of all orders.**

The "final objective" was the complete deportation of Jews from Poland.

[Source: Hochstadt, Steve, ed. *Sources of the Holocaust.* New York, NY: Palgrave Macmillan, 2004, pp. 87–88.]

the Nazis began exploiting the Jews in the ghettos as a source of forced labor. The Jews endured horrific living and working conditions, and death rates climbed as the population was ravaged by starvation and disease.

CHAPTER 3

EXTERMINATION IN THE EAST

In June of 1941, the Germans invaded the Soviet Union in an attack called Operation Barbarossa. The Wehrmacht was accompanied by four Einsatzgruppen assembled ahead of the invasion. Each Einsatzgruppe would operate within a specific geographic region: Einsatzgruppe A in Estonia, Latvia, and Lithuania; Einsatzgruppe B in Belarus, Einsatzgruppe C in Ukraine; and Einsatzgruppe D in Ukraine, the Crimea, and the Caucasus. Made up of between five hundred and one thousand personnel, each Einsatzgruppe was further divided into Sonderkommandos (Special Squads) and Einsatzkommandos (Action Squads). The Einsatzgruppen functioned independently of the Wehrmacht, which Hitler himself made clear in a directive, as quoted in Richard Rhodes's *Masters of Death*:

> **Within the field of operations of the army, in order to prepare the political and administrative organization, the *Reichsführer-SS* [Himmler] assumes on behalf of the Fuhrer special tasks which arise from the necessity finally to settle the conflict between two opposing political systems. Within the framework of these**

Invading Nazi forces approach a burning village in June 1941 during the opening days of Operation Barbarossa. The largest military operation launched by the Germans, the conflict in the Soviet Union would eventually claim more than twenty-six million Soviet casualties, thirteen million of which were civilians, according to some historians.

duties the *Reichsführer-SS* acts indepen-dently and on his own responsibility.

The two systems were Hitler's own Nazi ideology pitted against Joseph Stalin's Bolshevik government.

The genocide committed by the Einsatzgruppen involved in Operation Barbarossa marked the true beginning of the Holocaust. In Poland, in 1939, the Einsatzgruppen had nominally been enforcing security, although their atrocities became notorious. The Einsatzgruppen that operated in the Soviet Union functioned primarily as mobile killing units.

THE EINSATZGRUPPEN

The Einsatzgruppen drew from members of the Security Police and the Waffen SS. The leaders had been selected individually by Himmler and Heydrich, but most of the men learned only after their assignment to an Einsatzgruppe that they would be bound for the Soviet Union. Their orders were to execute the government officials and "extremist elements" in the newly occupied territory. Heydrich specified that they should target "Jews in the service of the party or government" and encourage anti-Jewish violence among the occupied population, but he made no mention of mass murder. In practice, however, it quickly became clear that Jews were the primary targets.

As the Wehrmacht advanced, encountering little initial resistance, the Einsatzgruppen followed a few days later. Soon after Einsatzgruppe A entered the Lithuanian city of Kaunas, they organized a pogrom, or massacre, of Jews at the hands of local collaborators. About 3,800 Jews were killed.

After the end of World War II, because of the thoroughness of the reports sent back to Berlin, war crimes prosecutors were easily able to establish the extent of the mass killings carried out by the Einsatzgruppen. One of the early accounts sent back tells of the situation in Kaunas, as printed in *The Einsatzgruppen Reports*:

> **On June 28 Vorkommando [an advance unit] has moved into Kaunas...During the night, exchange of heavy fire between Lithuanian insurgents, Jews, and irregulars. Very difficult to secure the prisons, which are totally overcrowded. During the last 3 days Lithuanian partisan groups have already killed several thousand Jews.**

Situations similar to the scenario in Kaunas were occurring across the occupied Soviet territory. The Einsatzgruppen operated out of larger cities, such as Riga, Latvia, and Minsk, Belorussia (Belarus), while sending out units into the surrounding countryside. Einsatzgruppen members encouraged violence by local collaborators and police, but they also executed Jews personally.

In midsummer of 1941, the orders to the Einsatzgruppen changed. "The vast area must be pacified as quickly as possible," Hitler said in a July meeting, as quoted by Rhodes. "The way to do that is to shoot dead anyone who even looks at us sideways." After this point, Himmler authorized large-scale massacres of Jews, now including women and children. (Official reports used the term "Jewess," which is widely considered derogatory today.) He also authorized Waffen-SS brigades and other forces to participate in the effort, bringing the total size of the force to thirty-six thousand. Commando units made up of local collaborators, especially soldiers and police, were also drawn up by the Nazis.

In 1941, about thirty-five thousand Jews lived in Kaunas, Lithuania. After the initial Nazi invasion and atrocities, the remaining Jews were forced to move into the district Slobodka, later called Kovno ghetto. Here, Jewish families move to the ghetto.

THE MASSACRE AT BABI YAR

Atrocities became routine for the Einsatzgruppen. Typically, they would arrive at a city or town and local collaborators would help them identify potential victims. Jews would be rounded up from their homes or they would be ordered to congregate in a centralized place, such as a market. In some cases, they were lured by the promise of work or told that they would be relocated. The victims were often unaware of their fate—they believed that they might be imprisoned but not killed. Sometimes they were executed publicly; other times, they would be forced to march or be taken by truck to a remote location. Mass graves would have been dug ahead of time, and small groups of victims would be lined up in front of the trenches and shot. Nazis and collaborators also looted their money, valuables, and sometimes even clothing.

Day by day, the tally of the dead rose. Karl Jäger, commander of Einsatzkommando 3 of Einsatzgruppe A, kept detailed totals of the mass killing he oversaw in Lithuania (excerpt from Rhodes):

Date	Place	Victims	Total
25–26.8.41	Seduva	230 Jews, 275 Jewesses, 159 Jewish children	664
26.8.41	Zarasai	767 Jews, 1,113 Jewesses, 1 Lith. Comm., 687 Jewish Children, 1 Russ. Comm. (f)	2,569
28.8.41	Pasvalys	402 Jews, 738 Jewesses, 209 Jewish Children	1,349

Through mid-September, Einsatzkommando 3 alone massacred 46,692 people. The other subunits also killed thousands or tens of thousands of victims.

The most notorious massacre perpetrated by the Einsatzgruppen occurred on September 29–30, 1941, at a ravine called Babi Yar outside of Kiev, Ukraine. On September 28, notices were posted ordering all of Kiev's Jews to assemble at a Jewish cemetery close to the mile-long ravine. They were told to bring their documents and valuables as well as warm clothing, and most believed that they were to be deported by train. A huge crowd assembled and were met by Sonderkommando 4a—part of Einsatzgruppe C—as well as units of local police and militia.

Victims entered a barbwire passage in groups of thirty or forty, leaving behind their belongings. Einsatzgruppe staff seated at desks took their valuables and discarded their papers. Ukrainian militia members herded the victims toward a field, beating them with clubs, and ordered them to undress. Past the field lay the ravine, and bodies of the dead and dying lay near the edge. Victims were ordered to lie down on top of the bodies, and then they were shot by gunmen.

Over the two days, 33,771 Jews were killed. A concentration camp was later set up near Babi Yar, and frequent executions at the site continued for the next year.

WIDESPREAD ATROCITIES

The Einsatzgruppen operated in the east throughout 1942, retreating in 1943. It is estimated that the Einsatzgruppen, along with other SS forces and collaborators, killed more than 1.3 million Jews over the course of the war. In addition, they targeted non-Jewish groups such as Communists,

"NEUROTICS OR BRUTES"

In mid-August of 1941, Himmler traveled to Belorussia to meet with SS leaders in the area. While there, he observed a massacre in Minsk in which between 120 and 190 victims were shot before pits that would be their graves. According to SS officer Erich von dem Bach-Zelewski, who accompanied Himmler, the SS chief had never seen anyone killed before. He was visibly nervous and skittish during the executions. During later testimony, Bach-Zelewski described urging him to consider the psychological effect of the killings on the executioners, as quoted in Rhodes's *Masters of Death*:

> **"Look at the men, how deeply shaken they are! Such men are finished for the rest of their lives! What kind of followers are we creating? Either neurotics or brutes!"**

Himmler later agreed that shooting was not the "most humane" method of mass murder, but his concern was for the killers, not the victims.

Gypsies, and the handicapped. The total number of the dead exceeded two million.

Despite the huge number of victims, Nazi leaders were not satisfied with the results of mass shootings in the east. Himmler, in particular, expressed concern over the mental health of the members of the Einsatzgruppen. The experience of killing defenseless fellow human beings created unspeakable psychological consequences. Some men experienced mental breakdowns and had to be institutionalized—Himmler set up mental hospitals for men who broke down after committing massacres. Others committed suicide. Alcohol abuse

An SS squad lines up Jews for execution at Babi Yar, a ravine in Kiev, Ukraine. Bodies of other victims lie in the ditch below them.

was rampant, and one officer mentioned delivering thousands of bottles of vodka to the men performing mass killings. Some became brutalized and came to enjoy the violence and death. Others distanced themselves from their own actions by claiming that despite having personal misgivings, they were just following orders.

Himmler authorized Arthur Nebe, head of Einsatzgruppe B, to investigate alternate methods of mass killing in 1941. Nebe experimented with dynamite and poison gas. Himmler subsequently ordered officials in Berlin to devise a van that would function as a mobile gas chamber. The Nazis had used gas vans before, but rekindled interest in poison gas led to a new round of experimentation and technical developments. In the autumn of 1941, the first gas vans—capable of holding between 80 and 150 people, depending on the size—were delivered to the Einsatzgruppen. The vehicles tended to break down, however, and the men disliked having to unload bodies from the interior. The gas vans were never widely used in the Soviet states.

Nazi leaders saw another disadvantage to mass killings in addition to the psychological burden: they were too public. Reports of the atrocities began to filter back to Germany.

The Nazis had not yet formally proposed the extermination of Europe's Jews in death camps, but the elements of the plan were in place. Jews were already confined to concentration camps and ghettos. The massacres by the Einsatzgruppen had set a precedent for mass killings. Research into poison gas provided a means of killing. As the atrocities became more and more monstrous, the Nazis were moving toward the Final Solution.

THE WANNSEE CONFERENCE

On January 20, 1942, fifteen high-ranking civil servants and Nazi Party officers gathered in a stately villa in the Berlin suburb of Wannsee. Today, their meeting is known as the Wannsee Conference. Most of the meeting consisted of a lecture by Reinhard Heydrich. Adolf Eichmann served as secretary. The summary of the meeting, edited by Heydrich, is known as the Wannsee Protocol. It is one of the key documents related to the evolution of the Nazis' plans for dealing with the Jews.

The topic under discussion was the Final Solution to the Jewish question. Anybody reading the protocol without background

Land		Zah
A. Altreich		131
Ostmark		43
Ostgebiete		420
Generalgouvernement		2.284
Bialystok		400
Protektorat Böhmen und Mähren		74
Estland	– judenfrei –	
Lettland		3
Litauen		34
Belgien		43
Dänemark		5
Frankreich / Besetztes Gebiet		165
Unbesetztes Gebiet		700
Griechenland		69
Niederlande		160
Norwegen		1
B. Bulgarien		48
England		330
Finnland		2
Irland		4
Italien einschl. Sardinien		58
Albanien		
Kroatien		40
Portugal		3
Rumänien einschl. Bessarabien		342
Schweden		8
Schweiz		18
Serbien		10
Slowakei		88
Spanien		6
Türkei (europ. Teil)		55
Ungarn		742
UdSSR		5.000
Ukraine	2.994.684	
Weißrußland ausschl. Bialystok	446.484	
Zusammen: über		11.000

K210405   372025

A reproduction of a page from the Wannsee Protocol lists the Jewish population of Europe by country. Heydrich anticipated exterminating Jews in areas as far-flung as Turkey and Ireland.

knowledge, however, might not recognize it as an outline of genocide. The document does not use the word "extermination" or even "kill." A key passage early in the text states that, "Another possible solution of the problem has now taken the place of emigration, i.e. the evacuation of the Jews to the East, provided that the Führer ['leader,' meaning Hitler] gives the appropriate approval." (The full document can be found at the Jewish Virtual Library research website.) The attendees at the meeting would have known that the phrase "evacuation to the east" was a euphemism for mass murder.

THE GENOCIDE MEETING

Heydrich stated the purpose of the meeting in the invitation he sent out to the attendees, as quoted by Mark Roseman in *The Wannsee Conference and the Final Solution*:

> **On July 31, 1941, the Reich Marshall of the Greater German Reich [Hermann Göring] commissioned me, with the assistance of the other central authorities, to make all necessary organizational and technical preparations for a comprehensive solution of the Jewish question and to present him with a comprehensive proposal at an early opportunity...**
>
> **Given the extraordinary significance of these questions and in the interest of achieving a common view among the central agencies involved in the relevant tasks, I propose to hold a meeting on these issues.**

Heydrich's guests, all high-level officials, included four SS officers and nine representatives of government

Heydrich was well qualified to plot out the Final Solution. Among other positions, he was chief of the RSHA, the security agency most directly involved in committing the Holocaust.

ministries, as well as Eichmann. Most belonged to departments that were involved in policy on Jewish matters in a legal, administrative, economic, or operational capacity. They represented the Ministries of the Interior and Justice, the Finance Ministry, the Ministry for the Occupied Eastern Territories, the Reich Chancellery, the Nazi Party Chancellery, the Foreign Office, and the SS Main Office for Race and Settlement.

Heydrich began by summarizing recent Nazi actions against the Jews, which the document describes as "struggle which has been carried on thus far against this enemy," and mentioned the "new solution." He then stated that "approximately eleven million Jews will be involved in the final solution of the European Jewish question." The document then lists the numbers of Jews affected in each country. In addition to nearby countries and regions, such as Austria, the former Poland, France, and the occupied Soviet states, the list also includes England, Turkey, and the Soviet Union. The huge geographic range demonstrates the far-reaching ambition of the Final Solution.

Heydrich did not specifically refer to the massacres being carried out in the Soviet Union. His list, however, referred to

Today, the villa where the Wannsee Conference took place is a museum, and the original Wannsee Protocol document is displayed in the room where Heydrich held the meeting.

Estonia as being "free of Jews," which tacitly acknowledged that the mass murder had already begun.

He then turned to the future:

> **In the course of the final solution the Jews are to be allocated for appropriate labor in the East. Ablebodied Jews, separated according to sex, will be taken in large work columns to these areas for work on roads, in the course of which action doubtless a large portion will be eliminated by natural causes. The possible final remnant will, since it will undoubtedly consist of the most resistant portion, have to be treated accordingly, because it is the product of natural selection and would, if released, act as the seed of a new Jewish revival.**

To put it simply, Jews would be worked to death or be killed. He went on to describe how Jews would be evacuated from the western regions to the east, beginning with Germany and Bohemia and Moravia.

Heydrich's final topic was a lengthy description of the fate of mixed-blood Jews and Jews in mixed marriages, reflecting the Nazis' obsession with racial purity. Some Jews may merely be sterilized rather than "evacuated." The meeting ended with discussion among the attendees, including "the different types of possible solutions" and the need to act quickly.

ORGANIZED MASS MURDER

The Wannsee Conference is sometimes described as the meeting in which the Final Solution was decided. That view

ZYKLON B

Five of the six death camps used the gas carbon monoxide for mass killings. Rudolf Höss decided instead to use the pesticide Zyklon B, as he described in testimony at the Nuremberg Trials after the war:

Highly poisonous and volatile, Zyklon B was supplied to Auschwitz in sealed metal containers. The chemical was initially developed for use as a disinfectant and insecticide.

The camp commandant at Treblinka... used monoxide gas, and I did not think that his methods were very efficient. So when I set up the extermination building at Auschwitz, I used Zyklon B, which was a crystallized prussic acid which we dropped into the death chamber from a small opening. It took from 3 to 15 minutes to kill the people in the death chamber, depending upon climatic conditions. We knew when the people were dead because their screaming stopped.

Prussic acid, also called hydrogen cyanide, releases poisonous cyanide gas that causes victims to asphyxiate.

Zyklon B was first tested at Auschwitz in September 1941, following Himmler's directive to find alternative methods of mass killings to shooting. The first victims were Soviet POWs, and at least one of the initial tests took place in the crematorium. It was subsequently converted into a gas chamber for periodic mass killings. Later on, several large gas chambers were constructed at Auschwitz.

A 1942 map shows the locations of many of the concentration camps and death camps in Poland. The document was originally published by an underground Polish resistance group.

is not entirely accurate—the genocide had already begun in the Soviet Union, and it was widely believed that Hitler had already authorized mass murder, perhaps a month or two earlier. Rather than decide on mass murder, the attendees discussed the details and implementation.

Nearly two decades later, during his trial for war crimes, Eichmann described the Wannsee Conference in interrogations and during his trial. He claimed that the language had been much more blunt during the discussion than was reported in the protocol. There had been actual discussion of killing and annihilation rather than the euphemistic language recorded afterward. However, Eichmann's testimony cannot be absolutely trusted because he was trying to portray himself as a minor player in the development of the Final Solution.

At the conference, the top Nazi and government officials were informed of the extent of the plan for genocide. This prepared them to issue appropriate orders and coordinate with other departments involved in the process. They were now all implicated in the Final Solution, and none of them had raised any objections on moral or humanitarian grounds.

THE AFTERMATH

Heydrich was satisfied with the outcome of his meeting. It had established his authority to administer the Final Solution and the fate of eleven million Jews. The other departments and ministries would be subordinate to the RSHA on the matter. In particular, the discussion had helped decide the fate of the Polish Jews. After the invasion of Poland, friction had arisen among Nazi leaders over the deportation of non-Germans into occupied Polish territory. At the Wannsee Conference, a government official representing occupied Poland volunteered for the Final Solution to begin with Polish Jews in the occupied territory, who were mainly "unfit for work."

After the meeting, Eichmann made thirty copies of the protocol and distributed them among the attendees and other top leaders. The conference catalyzed activity related to the Final Solution. Subsequent follow-up conferences held among lower-level officials addressed topics introduced at the Wannsee Conference, especially the matter of Jews of mixed blood or mixed marriages.

Many of the elements that made the Holocaust possible were now in place. The Wannsee Conference helped ensure future cooperation among the various departments of the Nazi bureaucracy. Mass killings had already begun, although they were not yet methodical and coordinated as would take place later on. The research into poison gas had revealed that a pesticide called Zyklon B could be used to produce highly toxic cyanide gas. Heydrich and Eichmann set to work planning a fresh wave of deportations.

Only one key factor in the preparation for the Final Solution was still missing: the extermination camps. But they were already being set up.

ENGINEERING THE DEATH CAMPS

I n early 1942, disquieting rumors began to circulate locally about activities being conducted by the Nazis near the town of Chelmno in occupied Poland. The SS had taken possession of a small villa and enclosed the site in a high fence guarded by sentries. Residents saw truckloads of prisoners being transported into the courtyard. In mid-January, an eyewitness reported what was going on inside, as quoted in Saul Friedländer's *The Years of Extermination*:

The place where all perish is called Chelmno, not far from Dabie, and all are hidden in the neighboring forest of Lochów. People are killed in two different ways: By firing squad or by poison gas...Lately thousands of Gypsies have been brought there from the so-called Gypsy camps of Lodz, and for the past several days, Jews have been brought there from Lodz and the same is done to them. Do not think that I am mad.

The killings began in Chelmno on December 6, 1941, more than a month before the Wannsee Conference convened. The facility was not constructed

Living conditions in many Jewish ghettos were miserable, leaving inhabitants struggling for survival. Here, a car has been converted into living quarters in the Kutno ghetto of Poland.

specifically as a death camp. The Nazis worked out of the villa, which also functioned as a reception area for the prisoners. The killings were done in three large gas vans rather than a stationary gas chamber. About a thousand victims could be killed in a day.

Most of the prisoners came from the nearby large city of Lodz, Poland, in which more than 150,000 Jews were confined to a ghetto. They were told that they were being deported for a work assignment, but they would instead be sent to Chelmno. After the victims were dead, the vans would transport the bodies into the forest, where they were buried in mass graves or burned. According to the U.S Holocaust Memorial Museum, at least 152,000 people, mostly Jews, were killed at Chelmno between 1941 and 1944.

Chelmno was one of the six death camps, or extermination camps, established for the sole purpose of mass murder. All were located in occupied Poland. They included Chelmno, Treblinka, Belzec, Sobibor, Majdanek, and Auschwitz-Birkenau.

PREPARING FOR SYSTEMATIC EXTERMINATION

Deportations accelerated in late 1941 in anticipation of the Final Solution, primarily under the administration of Eichmann. In Germany, the Jews had been stripped of their possessions, livelihoods, and dignity, but they had not been deported. In the autumn, however, deportations began of Jews from Germany as well as from Austria and the former Czechoslovakia. They were sent by train to Lodz and several sites in occupied Soviet territory, where most were housed in ghettos or held in concentration camps. Some, however, were shot and killed upon arrival.

Eichmann proved his efficiency by coordinating logistics concerning manpower, facilities, timetables, and train schedules. Tragically, Jewish community leaders often helped organize the deportations. Unaware of the impending Final Solution, many believed that resisting would only make the situation worse for the Jews.

The relocation was intended as a temporary measure. Construction of a second death camp was underway as the transports began. Belzec was a former Jewish work camp

German soldiers in the Kutno ghetto talk to a Jewish resident in 1940. Most of the ghetto's inhabitants were sent to the Chelmno death camp in 1942.

that had been unused for a year when SS officers returned with a crew of Polish laborers. The existence of the death camps was top secret—they were situated in remote locations and their purpose was concealed. The supervisor did not tell the Polish workers the ultimate purpose of a certain three-chambered small building that they constructed with metal-lined walls, heavy sealed doors, and a network of pipes under the floor. After the Polish workers finished their stint, a team of Ukranian prisoners of war (POWs) carried out further work at the site, including the completion of a short rail line as well as barbed-wire fences and a screen of trees. Jewish workers also worked on construction of the site.

In February 1942, the gas chamber was tested for the first time, with 150 Jewish workers the first victims. Killing operations began in March.

OPERATION REINHARD

Belzec was one of three death camps intended to exterminate the Jews from occupied Poland, a population that the Nazis estimated to be more than two million. The construction of Sobibor was finished in April, and Treblinka was completed in July. The death camps were all administered by the SS.

In June 1942, Reinhard Heydrich died of his injuries received in the May assassination attempt carried out by Czech resistance fighters. The mass killing of the Jews of occupied Poland at the Belzec, Sobibor, and Treblinka death camps was subsequently dubbed Operation Reinhard.

Many of the methods and procedures used across the death camps were first developed at Belzec. Jews were told that they were arriving at a transit camp, and they were unaware of their fate until moments before their death. The reception area was kept separate from the killing area. The prisoners were ordered to give up their valuables and undress. They were then forced to run through a passage into the gas chambers, which they were told were shower rooms. Some Jews from each transport were selected for the Sonderkommando, a "special unit" assigned work such as sorting possessions, cleaning rail cars, and transporting and burying bodies. The labor was only a temporary reprieve, and they were sent to the gas chambers after a month or two of work.

Belzec was closed in December 1942, Treblinka in August 1943, and Sobibor in October 1943. According to the U.S.

Jewish laborers are shown at Belzec in 1940. Before being converted into a death camp, Belzec was a work camp where inmates were forced to build fortifications and dig ditches.

Holocaust Memorial Museum, about 1,526,500 Jews lost their lives in the three camps. Most were from occupied Poland, but they were also deported from Germany, Austria, Czechoslovakia, the Netherlands, France, the Soviet Union, and other occupied territory. In addition, unknown numbers of Gypsies, Poles, and Soviet POWs were killed.

Operation Reinhard also encompassed several forced labor camps. Majdanek was constructed in 1941 as a Soviet POW and Jewish labor and concentration camp. It also contained gas chambers and functioned as a death camp, especially after Belzec was shut down. In late 1943, the last desperate inmates at Sobibor and Treblinka mounted uprisings. Apprehensive about the possibility of such an uprising in Majdanek, SS leaders decided to execute the remaining Jews. On November 3, more than eighteen thousand Jews were shot in the largest mass killing in one place that occurred during the Holocaust. The killing lasted for days, with forty-two thousand to forty-three thousand Jews murdered by the end. The so-called Harvest Festival brought Operation Reinhard to an end.

THE HORRORS OF AUSCHWITZ

Auschwitz was the largest of all of the Nazi concentration camp complexes. The original concentration camp was set up in 1940 at the site of a former Polish artillery base. It was expanded in 1941, and the newer, much larger camp became known as Birkenau or Auschwitz II. A third complex consisted of a massive forced labor camp where prisoners worked in factories for German companies that included I. G. Farben. The prisoners of Auschwitz experienced indescribable misery, enduring horrendous conditions in the labor camps, being subjected to medical experimentation, and receiving barely enough food for survival. Above all, however, Auschwitz has become infamous for its large-scale mass killings of Jews in its gas chambers.

Early in 1942, plans were made for the construction of a new, larger crematorium. The initial drawings show that although it could function as both a gas chamber and crematorium, it would have been too small to perform large-scale mass killings. But the Nazis' plans were to change. In mid-1942, two improvised gas chambers were set up in nearby houses. Auschwitz had become a death camp. By the time

RUDOLF HÖSS

As camp commandant of Auschwitz from 1940 to 1943, Rudolf Höss presided over history's most extensive mass murder. He learned the concentration camp system while working at Dachau from 1934 to 1938, and he applied many of the same structures and principles to Auschwitz. Dachau was notorious for breaking inmates through physical and mental torture. Auschwitz was worse. After it was decided that Birkenau would be established as a death camp, Höss was responsible for setting up the installations and techniques that made possible the efficient killing of over a million people.

After the war, he offered testimony about his own perspective and about his superiors:

DR. KAUFFMANN: Did you yourself ever feel pity with the victims, thinking of your own family and children?

HÖSS: Yes.

DR. KAUFFMANN: How was it possible for you to carry out these actions in spite of this?

HÖSS: In view of all these doubts which I had, the only one and decisive argument was the strict order and the reason given for it by the Reichsführer Himmler.

DR. KAUFFMANN: I ask you whether Himmler inspected the camp and convinced himself, too, of the process of annihilation?

HÖSS: Yes. Himmler visited the camp in 1942 and he watched in detail one processing from beginning to end.

> **DR. KAUFMANN:** Does the same apply to Eichmann?
>
> **HÖSS:** Eichmann came repeatedly to Auschwitz and was intimately acquainted with the proceedings.

construction in Birkenau finally began later in the year, the plans included four massive crematoria connected to gas chambers that had the capacity to kill more than four thousand people every day. They were completed in mid-1943.

Massive killing operations began at Birkenau after the Operation Reinhard death camps had been shut down. The killings accelerated in 1944 as the Allies gained ground and Nazi forces retreated from the territory they had invaded. Jews were moved out of the ghettos and labor camps. More than four hundred thousand Jews were transported to Auschwitz from Hungary alone.

Upon arriving at Auschwitz, some prisoners would be taken to labor camps, while most would be sent directly to their deaths. As in the other death camps, much of the worst work was done by Jews recruited in the Sonderkommando. The size of the unit was increased to 874 men in mid-1944 because of the extent of the killings being carried out at Auschwitz. They were forbidden to tell the prisoners what awaited them in the so-called shower rooms. Sonderkommando worker Filip Müller later described the arrival of deportees, as quoted in *Sources of the Holocaust*:

> **I was able to catch a few words and learned that these people had been working in a factory. From there they were deported**

Prisoners in Auschwitz were crowded into barracks, such as this one for women, which lacked heat or adequate sanitary facilities. Many who were spared the gas chambers died of starvation, disease, or forced labor.

quite suddenly, supposedly for important work using their special skills...

Would anything have been changed in the course of events if any of us had stepped out and, facing the crowd, had shouted: "Do not be deceived, men and women, you are taking your last walk, a terrible death in the gas chambers awaits you!"

The prisoners were told by the guard that they had to undress to be disinfected

The bodies of victims at Auschwitz were burned in huge ovens for cremating. After the construction of several new crematoria in 1943, thousands of corpses could be destroyed every day.

in showers. Once the people were locked inside the chamber, poison gas crystals were dropped within and loud trucks were turned nearby.

Their noise was to prevent anyone in the camp from hearing the shouting and the banging on the doors of the dying in the gas chamber. We, however, were spared nothing, but had to witness everything in close proximity. It was as though Judgment Day had come. We could clearly hear heart-rending weeping, cries for help, fervent prayers, violent banging and knocking...

The killings at Auschwitz continued until November 1944. The victims were mainly Jews from Hungary, Poland, Czechoslovakia, France, the Netherlands, Greece, and Belgium. Other victims included Poles, Gypsies, and Soviet POWs. In total, at least 960,000 Jews and 120,000 non-Jews were killed at Auschwitz according to the U.S. Holocaust Memorial Museum.

CHAPTER 6

FINAL RECKONING

German forces ceased advancing in 1942, and by 1943, the tide of the war had turned against the Nazis. As the fighting continued on the front and Allied bombings of Germany left many German cities crippled or devastated, some Nazi leaders turned their attention to concealing the evidence of the atrocities committed against the Jews.

Shortly before his death, Heydrich assigned the Einsatzgruppen the task of revisiting the sites of their massacres and destroying all traces of the mass murder that had occurred. The campaign was eventually given the code name Aktion 1005. Paul Blobel, commander of one of the Einsatzgruppe Sonderkommandos, exhumed bodies from mass graves at Chelmno to experiment with the best methods of destroying corpses. In May 1943, Blobel and a newly formed Sonderkommando began exhuming and burning bodies across occupied Soviet territory. Much of the work was done by Jewish forced laborers who were in turn executed and burned on the bonfires.

The facilities at Belzec, Sobibor, and Treblinka were all destroyed after Operation Reinhard ended. The bodies at the sites were exhumed and burned as part of Aktion 1005. The ground was plowed under and planted with crops in an attempt to create the appearance of a farm. At Belzec, the Germans even constructed a manor house.

Auschwitz continued operating nearly until the end of the war. In August and September 1944, the Allied forces bombed the industrial complex of the camp. They did not, however, target the gas chambers even though leaders had already received detailed reports about the mass killings. The fact that the Allies failed even to attempt bombing the death camp remains controversial to this day.

After mass killings ceased in November, the gas chambers, crematoria, and other installations related to the mass killings were dismantled. The incineration trenches and mass burial

A bone crushing machine is shown in 1944. Paul Blobel, who led early operations to erase evidence of mass killings, developed systematic methods of destroying bodies and scattering the ashes.

pits were bulldozed. In mid-January, as the Soviet forces drew nearer, the Nazis began evacuating the concentration camp. Nearly sixty thousand prisoners were forced to leave Auschwitz in what was for many a death march. The Soviets liberated Auschwitz on January 27, 1945.

FALL OF THE THIRD REICH

On May 7, 1945, Germany surrendered unconditionally. Hitler, hiding in a secure bunker, had taken his own life on

THE NAZI HUNTERS

Only a small proportion of the war criminals who perpetrated the Holocaust were brought to justice. Many more fled and went into hiding after the end of the war. The effort to track down and prosecute these criminals is ongoing even into the twenty-first century.

The best known "Nazi hunter" was Simon Wiesenthal (1908–2005), who survived being held in forced labor camps and concentration camps throughout the war. In 1947, he founded the Jewish Historical Documentation Center in Austria. Wiesenthal provided information that helped in the capture of war criminals such as Adolf Eichmann; Franz Stangl, commandant of Sobibor and Treblinka; and Karl Silberbauer, the Gestapo officer who arrested Anne Frank (who wrote *The Diary of a Young Girl*) and her family.

In the United States, the hunt for Nazis was led by the Office of Special Investigations (OSI), a unit within the Department of Justice that identified more than a hundred Nazi war criminals. The OSI is now part of the Human Rights and Special Prosecutions Section.

April 30 as Soviet forces prepared to enter Berlin. He remained unrepentant and vitriolic until the end, stating in his "Political Testament" composed the previous day that he was not to blame for the war: "The real people to blame for this murderous struggle would be: the Jews!" (as quoted in Richard Evans's *The Third Reich at War*).

The other remaining top Nazi leaders also had to decide whether to choose suicide, surrender, or attempt escape. Hermann Göring gave himself up to American forces. He was put on trial and condemned to death, but he killed himself with a poison capsule before the sentence was carried out.

Himmler retained considerable power within the Third Reich nearly to the end. He was appointed Minister of the Interior in 1943, giving him authority over the courts and civil service. After a failed attempt on Hitler's life in 1944 by a conspiracy within the German army, Himmler was given more control over military affairs. In April 1945, however, Himmler recognized that defeat was imminent and attempted to negotiate with the Allies. His move enraged Hitler, who stripped him of all offices of state.

Himmler attempted to flee carrying forged papers. On May 21, he was detained at a checkpoint manned by Soviet POWs who handed him over to the British without knowing his identity. Himmler gave the British his real name and cooperated with interrogators, but he killed himself by biting down on a cyanide capsule concealed in his mouth soon after being taken into custody.

With Hitler's death, the Nazi Party collapsed. Germany passed into the control of Allied forces with little resistance from its citizens. Only gradually did the world become aware of the deaths of the millions of Jews who had been annihilated during the earlier years of the war.

As Allied forces neared Berlin in 1945, Adolf Hitler retreated to an underground bunker, an eighteen-room air raid shelter beneath his Berlin residence. Nazi troops destroyed the bunker's command center and its documents after Hitler's suicide.

SEEKING JUSTICE

In 1945, the International Military Tribunal was convened in Nuremberg, Germany, presided over by military judges from the Soviet Union, Great Britain, France, and the United States. Its purpose was to punish the war criminals who had committed atrocities against civilians. Possible charges brought against the accused included crimes against peace, war crimes, crimes against humanity, and conspiracy to commit the three crimes. The most high-profile conviction was that of Hermann Göring, who was found guilty on all four counts. Hans Frank, the governor general of occupied Poland, was also convicted on two counts and executed in 1946. In 1947, twenty-two Einsatzgruppen commanders and officers received convictions at Nuremberg. Some sentences were later reduced, but four defendants, including Paul Blobel, were hanged.

Historical footage of the Nuremberg Trials still exists and shows the courtroom proceedings in which prosecutors state their cases, the accused war criminals offer testimony, and victims speak about their experiences. In 1948, the U.S. Department of Defense completed a powerful documentary called *Nuremberg: Its Lesson for Today*, which included graphic footage of Nazi atrocities as well as courtroom scenes. It was not released in the United States until 2012.

During the series of trials, which took place between 1945 and 1949, 186 Nazi perpetrators were convicted. The tribunal set a new precedent for international cooperation in pursuing justice, but many Nazi war criminals escaped prosecution at Nuremburg. In some cases, they were later brought to trial in national courts of law. Rudolf Höss, for example, escaped using a false identity after the end of the war and was finally captured in 1946. He was brought before the Nuremberg tribunal as a witness, but he was tried and sentenced to death for his crimes in a Polish court. Höss was hanged in Auschwitz in 1947.

"THE BANALITY OF EVIL"

After the Wannsee Conference, Eichmann was instrumental in coordinating the deportations of Jews from across Europe

Rudolf Hess *(second from left)* leans on the bench during proceedings at the Nuremberg Trials. Also shown in the defendants' dock are Hermann Göring, Joachim von Ribbentrop, and Wilhelm Keitel.

to the death camps. He was captured by the Americans after the war ended, but he gave a fake name and escaped custody in 1946, fleeing to Argentina. He lived outside Buenos Aires for fourteen years until the Israeli Security Service tracked him down, abducted him, and brought him to Jerusalem for trial.

The highly publicized trial lasted four months. Testimony by Holocaust survivors was highly emotional, and Eichmann sat in a bulletproof glass box during the proceedings. In the end, he was found guilty of crimes against humanity, crimes

Standing in the prisoner's cage, Adolf Eichmann listens to the reading of the indictment against him at his 1961 trial for war crimes, held in Jerusalem.

against the Jewish people, and other charges such as membership in the Gestapo, a criminal organization. He was sentenced to death and hanged in 1962.

The most famous account of the trial appeared in Hannah Arendt's book *Eichmann in Jerusalem: A Report on the Banality of Evil*. Like many spectators, Arendt was struck by how ordinary Eichmann appeared:

> **When I speak of the banality of evil, I do so only on the strictly factual level, pointing to a phenomenon which stared one in the face at the trial...Except for an extraordinary diligence in looking out for his personal advancement, he had no motives at all...That such remoteness from reality and such thoughtlessness can wreak more havoc than all the evil instincts taken together which, perhaps, are inherent in man—that was, in fact, the lesson one could learn in Jerusalem.**

Arendt's contentions sparked great controversy. Many historians and scholars disagreed with her depiction of the "desk murderer." But today, aspects of the Holocaust, its perpetrators, and the events that led to the Final Solution are still undergoing constant reevaluation and fresh analysis. In a sense, just as museums and monuments ensure that the victims will not be forgotten, the historical examination of the subject serves as an ongoing tribute to the millions lost in the Holocaust.

Timeline

January 30, 1933 Adolf Hitler is appointed chancellor of Germany.

September 15, 1935 Nazi leaders announce the Nuremberg Laws.

June 17, 1936 Hitler appoints Heinrich Himmler Reichsführer SS and chief of German police.

March 11, 1938 German troops invade Austria and incorporate Austria into the German Reich.

November 9–10, 1938 The Nazis vandalize Jewish homes, businesses, synagogues, and schools and attack Jews during Kristallnacht, "The Night of Broken Glass."

September 1, 1939 Germany invades Poland, initiating World War II in Europe.

September 27, 1939 Himmler combines the Security Police and the SD into Reich Security Main Office (RSHA), the agency that will implement the Final Solution.

May 20, 1940 SS authorities establish Auschwitz, the largest concentration camp complex of the Nazi regime and later the largest death camp.

June 22, 1941 Germany launches Operation Barbarossa, the invasion of the Soviet Union. The Einsatzgruppen follow behind the army and commit mass killings of Jews and non-Germans.

July 31, 1941 Hermann Göring authorizes Reinhard Heydrich to coordinate a "total solution of the Jewish Question" in Europe.

September 3, 1941 The poison gas Zyklon B is first tested at Auschwitz with the killings of Soviet POWs.

December 8, 1941 Killing operations begin at Chelmno, the first death camp.

January 20, 1942 Heydrich convenes the Wannsee Conference to discuss and coordinate the Final Solution.

March–July 1942 The Operation Reinhard death camps—Belzec, Sobibor, and Treblinka—begin killing operations.

May 27, 1942 Czech resistance fighters bomb Heydrich's car, inflicting fatal injuries.

December 1942–October 1943 The Operation Reinhard death camps are closed.

March–June 1943 The construction of four large crematoria enables massive killing operations to begin at Auschwitz.

November 3, 1943 Tens of thousands of Jews are killed in the "Harvest Festival" at Majdanek.

November 25, 1944 Himmler orders the destruction of the killing facilities at Auschwitz.

April 30, 1945 Hitler commits suicide in his bunker in Berlin.

May 7, 1945 German forces surrender unconditionally to the Allies.

May 23, 1945 Himmler commits suicide while in custody of British forces.

November 20, 1945 The International Military Tribunal convenes at Nuremberg.

April 1961 Adolf Eichmann is put on trial in Jerusalem.

Glossary

ANNEX To incorporate territory into a political unit.

ANNIHILATION The utter destruction of the collective existence or main body of something, as an army or group of people.

ANTI-SEMITISM Hostility toward or discrimination against Jews.

ATROCITY An act of extreme cruelty or violence, especially during wartime.

COLLABORATOR One who cooperates with the enemy of one's nation during war, especially occupying forces.

CONCENTRATION CAMP A prison camp in which opponents of the Nazis were held without trial.

CREMATORIUM A furnace in which bodies of the dead are burned to ashes.

DEPORT To expel or banish from a country.

DICTATOR A ruler holding absolute power without restriction by a constitution or laws.

DISCRIMINATION Prejudicial treatment of members of a certain group based on class, religion, race, gender, or sexual orientation.

EXECUTE To put to death, often as punishment for a crime or in accordance with the law.

EXHUME To dig up, especially a person's dead body that was buried.

EXTERMINATION The killing of a person or group of people.

GENOCIDE The deliberate and systematic destruction of a racial, national, or cultural group.

GHETTO A city section where Jews were required to live under the Nazi regime.

MASSACRE The indiscriminate killing of a large number of usually helpless or unresisting victims.

MILITIA A body of citizen soldiers, as opposed to professional soldiers.

PERPETRATOR One who commits a crime or other harmful act.

TESTIMONY A sworn statement given by a witness, usually in court.

WAR CRIME An act committed during wartime that violates international agreements.

For More Information

Foundation Memorial to the Murdered Jews of Europe
Executive Office
Georgenstraße 23
10117 Berlin
Germany
Website: http://www.holocaust-mahnmal.de/en
The objective of the foundation is to remember the
    National Socialist genocide of European Jewry and
    ensure that all victims of the National Socialist regime
    are honored appropriately.

Montreal Holocaust Memorial Centre
5151, chemin de la Côte-Sainte-Catherine
(Cummings House)
Montréal, QC H3W 1M6
Canada
(514) 345-2605
Website: http://www.mhmc.ca/en
The Montreal Holocaust Memorial Centre educates peo-
    ple of all ages and backgrounds about the Holocaust,
    while sensitizing the public to the universal perils of
    anti-Semitism, racism, hate, and indifference.

Simon Wiesenthal Center
1399 South Roxbury Drive
Los Angeles, CA 90035
(310) 553-9036
Website: http://www.wiesenthal.com

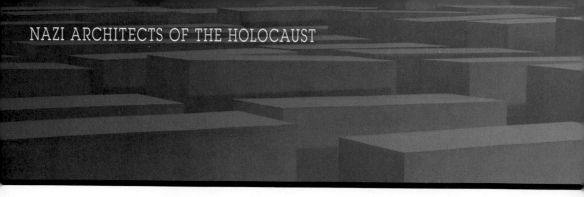

The Simon Wiesenthal Center is a global Jewish human rights organization that confronts anti-Semitism, hate, and terrorism; promotes human rights and dignity; stands with Israel; defends the safety of Jews worldwide; and teaches the lessons of the Holocaust for future generations.

U.S. Holocaust Memorial Museum
100 Raoul Wallenberg Place SW
Washington, DC 20024-2126
(202) 488-0400
Website: http://www.ushmm.org
The U.S. Holocaust Memorial Museum is America's national institution for the documentation, study, and interpretation of Holocaust history and serves as the country's memorial to the millions of people murdered during the Holocaust.

Vancouver Holocaust Education Centre
50–950 West 41st Avenue
Vancouver, BC V5Z 2N7
Canada
(604) 264-0499
Website: http://www.vhec.org
The mission of the Vancouver Holocaust Education Centre is to promote human rights, social justice, and genocide awareness and teach about the causes and consequences

of discrimination, racism, and anti-Semitism through education and remembrance of the Holocaust.

Voice/Vision Holocaust Survivor Oral History Archive
University of Michigan-Dearborn
Mardigian Library
4901 Evergreen Road
Dearborn, MI 48128-1491
(313) 583-6300
Website: http://holocaust.umd.umich.edu
The Voice/Vision Archive promotes cultural, racial, and religious understanding through unprecedented world-wide access to its collection of Holocaust survivor narratives.

Wiener Library for the Study of the Holocaust and Genocide
29 Russell Square
London, WC1B 5DP
England
Website: http://www.wienerlibrary.co.uk
The Wiener Library is one of the world's leading and most extensive archives on the Holocaust and Nazi era. Formed in 1933, the library's unique collection of over one million items includes published and unpublished works, press cuttings, photographs, and eyewitness testimony.

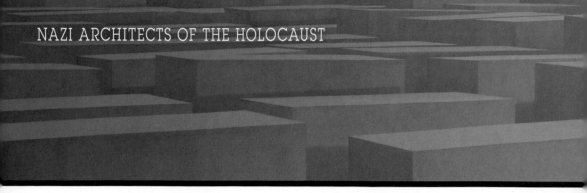

Yad Vashem
Holocaust Martyrs' and Heroes' Remembrance Authority
P.O. Box 3477
Jerusalem 9103401
Israel
Website: http://www.yadvashem.org
Israel's official memorial to the Jewish victims of the
  Holocaust, Yad Vashem is a world center for documen-
  tation, research, education, and commemoration of
  the Holocaust.

WEBSITES

Due to the changing nature of Internet links, Rosen
Publishing has developed an online list of websites related
to the subject of this book. This site is updated regularly.
Please use this link to access the list:

http://www.rosenlinks.com/DHH/Arch

For Further Reading

Altman, Linda Jacobs. *The Warsaw Ghetto Uprising: Striking a Blow Against the Nazis*. Berkeley Heights, NJ: Enslow Publishers, 2012.

Bard, Mitchell Geoffrey. *48 Hours of Kristallnacht: Night of Destruction/Dawn of the Holocaust: An Oral History*. Guilford, CT: Lyons Press, 2008.

Bascomb, Neal. *Hunting Eichman: How a Band of Survivors and a Young Spy Agency Chased Down the World's Most Notorious Nazi*. Boston, MA: Mariner Books, 2010.

Bergen, Doris L. *War and Genocide: A Concise History of the Holocaust*. Lanham, MD: Rowman & Littlefield Publishers, 2009.

Frank, Anne. *The Diary of a Young Girl*. New York, NY: Alfred A. Knopf, 2010.

Jackson, Livia Bitton. *I Have Lived a Thousand Years: Growing Up in the Holocaust*. New York, NY: Simon & Schuster, 1999.

Levi, Primo. *Survival in Auschwitz*. Radford, VA: Wilder Publications, 2011.

Megargee, Geoffrey P., ed. *The United States Holocaust Memorial Museum Encyclopedia of Camps and Ghettos, 1933–1945: Ghettos in German-Occupied Eastern Europe*. Bloomington, IN: Indiana University Press, 2012.

Müller, Filip. *Eyewitness Auschwitz: Three Years in the Gas Chambers*. Chicago, IL: Ivan R. Dee, 1999.

Price, Sean. *Adolf Hitler*. New York, NY: Franklin Watts, 2010.

Roland, Paul. *The Nuremberg Trials: The Nazis and Their Crimes Against Humanity*. Edison, NJ: Chartwell Books, 2010.

Shirer, William L. *The Rise and Fall of the Third Reich*. New York, NY: Simon & Schuster, 2011.

Soumerai, Eve Nussbaum, and Carol D. Schulz. *Daily Life During the Holocaust*. Westport, CT: Greenwood Press, 2009.

Speer, Albert. *Inside the Third Reich: Memoirs*. Bronx, NY: Ishi Press, 2009.

Spiegelman, Art. *The Complete Maus: A Survivor's Tale*. New York, NY: Pantheon Books, 1996.

Stahel, David. *Operation Barbarossa and Germany's Defeat in the East*. New York, NY: Cambridge University Press, 2009.

Weale, Adrian. *Army of Evil: A History of the SS*. New York, NY: NAL Caliber, 2012.

Wiesel, Elie. *Night*. New York, NY: Hill and Wang, 2006.

Wood, Angela. *Holocaust: The Events and Their Impact on Real People*. New York, NY: DK Publishing, 2007.

Zusak, Markus. *The Book Thief*. New York, NY: Alfred A. Knopf, 2007.

Bibliography

Arad, Yitzhak, Shmuel Krakowski, and Shmuel Spector,
 eds. *The Einsatzgruppen Reports*. New York, NY: Holocaust
 Library, 1989.

Arendt, Hannah. *Eichmann in Jerusalem: A Report on the
 Banality of Evil*. New York, NY: Penguin Books, 1992.

Benz, Wolfgang. *The Holocaust: A German Historian
 Examines the Genocide*. New York, NY: Columbia
 University Press, 1999.

Bowcott, Owen. "Restored Film Gives Fresh Insight into
 Trials of Nazi War Criminals." *Guardian*, February 23,
 2012. Retrieved September 19, 2013 (http://www.the
 guardian.com/law/2012/feb/23/nuremberg-trials-filmed).

Browning, Christopher R. *The Origins of the Final Solution:
 The Evolution of Nazi Jewish Policy, September 1939–
 March 1942*. Lincoln, NB: University of Nebraska
 Press, 2004.

Cesarani, David. *Becoming Eichmann: Rethinking the Life, Crimes
 and Trial of a "Desk Murderer."* Cambridge, MA: Da Capa
 Press, 2004.

Dawidowicz, Lucy S. *The War Against the Jews 1933–1945*.
 New York, NY: Bantam Books, 1986.

Evans, Richard J. *The Third Reich at War*. New York, NY:
 The Penguin Press, 2009.

Friedländer, Saul. *The Years of Extermination: Nazi Germany
 and the Jews 1939–1945*. New York, NY: HarperCollins
 Publishers, 2006.

Gerwarth, Robert. *Hitler's Hangman: The Life of Heydrich*.
 New Haven, CT: Yale University Press, 2011.

Gilbert, Martin. *The Holocaust: A History of the Jews of Europe During the Second World War*. New York, NY: Holt, Rinehart and Winston, 1985.

Hartmann, Christian. *Operation Barbarossa: Nazi Germany's War in the East, 1941–1945*. Oxford, UK: Oxford University Press, 2013.

Hitler, Adolf. *Mein Kampf*. A Project Gutenberg of Australia eBook, 2002. Retrieved September 19, 2013 (http://gutenberg.net.au/ebooks02/0200601.txt).

Hochstadt, Steve, ed. *Sources of the Holocaust*. New York, NY: Palgrave Macmillan, 2004.

Jewish Virtual Library. "The 'Final Solution': The Wannsee Protocol." 2013. Retrieved October 8, 2013 (http://www.jewishvirtuallibrary.org/jsource/Holocaust/Wannsee_Protocol.html).

Kershaw, Ian. *Hitler, the Germans and the Final Solution*. New Haven, CT: Yale University Press, 2008.

Laqueur, Walter, ed. *The Holocaust Encyclopedia*. New Haven, CT: Yale University Press, 2001.

Library of Congress "Trial of the Major War Criminals Before the International Military Tribunal Nuremberg, 14 November 1945–1 October 1946." Retrieved September 19, 2013 (http://www.loc.gov/rr/frd/Military_Law/NT_major-war-criminals.html).

Longerich, Peter. *Heinrich Himmler*. New York, NY: Oxford University Press, 2012.

Rees, Laurence. *Auschwitz: A New History*. New York, NY: PublicAffairs, 2005.

Rhodes, Richard. *Masters of Death: The SS Einsatzgruppen and the Invention of the Holocaust.* New York, NY: Alfred A. Knopf, 2002.

Roseman, Mark. *The Wannsee Conference and the Final Solution: A Reconsideration.* New York, NY: Metropolitan Books, 2002.

Rozett, Robert, and Shmuel Spector, eds. *Encyclopedia of the Holocaust.* New York, NY: Facts On File, 2000.

U.S. Holocaust Memorial Museum. "Holocaust Encyclopedia." 2014. Retrieved September 19, 2013 (http://www.ushmm.org/learn/holocaust-encyclopedia).

Index

ABOUT THE AUTHOR

Corona Brezina has written more than a dozen young adult books. Several of her previous books have also focused on topics related to history and political science, including *Primary Sources of Political Systems: Dictatorship* and *The Treaty of Versailles*. She lives in Chicago, Illinois.

PHOTO CREDITS

Cover (top) Picture Post/Getty Images; cover (center) © iStockphoto .com/Steve Christensen; cover (bottom), pp. 42, 44 Hugo Jaeger /Time & Life Pictures/Getty Images; pp. 4–5, 24, 32, 35 © AP Images; p. 8 Roger Viollet/Getty Images; p. 11 Pantheon/SuperStock; pp. 12, 18 Keystone-France/Gamma-Keystone/Getty Images; pp. 15, 17 Imagno/Hulton Archive/Getty Images; p. 21 AFP/Getty Images; p. 26 United States Holocaust Memorial Museum, courtesy of the Abraham and Ruth Goldfarb Family Acquisition Fund; p. 30 Hulton Archive/Getty Images; p. 34 Universal Images Group/Getty Images; p. 37 (inset) CTK/AP Images; p. 38 Galerie Bilderwelt /Hulton Archive/Getty Images; p. 46 United States Holocaust Memorial Museum, Muzeum Regionalne w Tomaszow Lubelski; p. 50 Forum/Universal Images Group/Getty Images; p. 51 Gabriel Hackett/Hulton Archive/Getty Images; p. 54 United States Holocaust Memorial Museum, courtesy of Herman Lewinter; p. 57 William Vandivert/Time & Life Pictures/Getty Images; p. 59 Central Press /Hulton Archive/Getty Images; p. 60 Gjon Mili/Time & Life Pictures/Getty Images; cover and interior page background elements optimarc/Shutterstock.com (gray textures), Gallup Pix/Photodisc /Thinkstock (pillars), Gubin Yury/Shutterstock.com (barbed wire).

Designer: Brian Garvey; Editor: Kathy Kuhtz Campbell; Photo Researcher: Cindy Reiman